International Training
Corporation

T0318979

EFFECTIVE PRESENTATION SKILLS

Jossey-Bass
Pfeiffer
San Francisco

A training system designed by International Training Corporation

Copyright © 1993 by International Training Corporation

ISBN: 088390-366-0

These written materials are to be used only in conjunction with associated video presentations.

Clients have agreed by purchasing video material that each viewer of the presentation(s) will be provided with a set of associated written material(s) for each individual viewer's sole use.

Published by

International Training Corporation
357 Winston Ave., NE
North Canton, Ohio 44720
(216) 966-1170

 350 Sansome Street, 5th Floor
San Francisco, California 94104-1342
(415) 433-1740; Fax (415) 433-0499
(800) 274-4434; Fax (800) 569-0443

Visit our website at: www.pfeiffer.com

Printing   10   9

 This book is printed on acid-free, recycled stock that meets or exceeds the minimum GPO and EPA requirements for recycled paper.

TABLE OF CONTENTS

MODULE 1: *PLANNING THE PRESENTATION*

MODULE 2: *PREPARING THE PRESENTATION*

MODULE 3: *THE DELIVERY*

MODULE 1:
Planning the Presentation
UNIT 1
The Planning Process
Overview

Introduction   Some people think that they can deliver effective presentations without planning. Experienced presenters know that they need to plan the presentation and anticipate situations that may occur.

Some of the major benefits of planning your presentation include:

- polished delivery skills;
- the ability to give a presentation within a time limit;
- anticipation of the audience's comfort;
- the ability to alter a presentation to meet various needs; and
- a reduction of technical problems.

The phrase, "An ounce of planning is worth a pound of excuses" speaks to the difference between successful and unsuccessful presenters.

Unit objectives   When you complete this unit, you will be able to:

- identify the purpose of a presentation;
- write a purpose statement;
- explain why analyzing an audience is important; and
- complete an audience analysis worksheet.

Topics   This unit covers the following topics:

- Identifying the Purpose of a Presentation; and
- Analyzing the Audience.

Video Exercise: Great Speeches—Martin Luther King, Jr.

Martin Luther King, Jr.
"I Have a Dream"
Washington, DC
August, 1963

Directions
Evaluate Reverend King's speech. Write down the presentation techniques that help make this a great speech.

Background
A leader in the Southern Christian Leadership Conference, Reverend King preached passive resistance. He launched his campaign against segregation with the Montgomery Bus Boycott.

His response to hatred was love and this attitude launched him into national prominence. Receiving the Nobel Peace Prize provided him with the credentials to become a spokesperson for racial equality.

When he addressed over 200,000 people at the Lincoln Memorial in 1963, he touched the audience with the sincerity of his convictions, vision, and faith. "I Have a Dream" is a speech that continues to move all those who hear it.

Notes

_____
_____
_____
_____
_____
_____
_____
_____
_____
_____
_____
_____
_____
_____
_____
_____
_____

Video Exercise: Great Speeches—Winston Churchill

Winston Churchill
"Some Chicken Speech"
Canadian Parliament
1940

Directions

Evaluate the Prime Minister's speech. Write down the presentation techniques that help make this a great speech. Note his use of metaphors and timing.

Background

Winston Churchill was one of the great orators of the 20th century. His rise to power was spurred by his demands for rearmament during World War II and his challenge to Chamberlain's appeasement of Hitler at Munich in 1938.

Churchill became Prime Minster of the United Kingdom in 1940.

Notes

_____

_____

_____

_____

_____

_____

_____

_____

_____

_____

_____

_____

_____

_____

_____

_____

_____

_____

_____

Video Exercise: Great Speeches—Rep. Barbara Jordan

Representative Barbara Jordan
"Keynote Address"
Democratic Convention
July 12, 1976

Directions Evaluate Representative Jordan's speech. Write down the presentation techniques that help make this a great speech. Note her clear articulation, effective pace, and majestic voice quality.

Background

Every four years, political parties seek effective speakers to deliver the keynote convention addresses. These speakers have elegance, stature, name recognition, the ability to motivate audiences, and star appeal.

A graduate of Texas Southern University where she was a noted debater, Barbara Jordan completed her law studies at Boston University. Elected to the U.S. House of Representatives, Barbara Jordan gained national prominence during the Watergate hearings.

In 1976, Representative Jordan became the first black woman to deliver a keynote address at a national political convention.

Notes

_____
_____
_____
_____
_____
_____
_____
_____
_____
_____
_____
_____
_____
_____
_____
_____
_____
_____
_____

Video Exercise: Great Speeches—John F. Kennedy

John F. Kennedy
"Inaugural Address"
Washington, DC.
January 20, 1963

Directions   Evaluate President Kennedy's speech. Write down the presentation techniques that help make this a great speech. Note his eloquent delivery style, phrasing, and pauses.

Background   John F. Kennedy was a graduate of Harvard University, and a recipient of the Purple Heart and the Navy and Marine Corps Medal. In 1952, Kennedy defeated Henry Cabot Lodge and became a Senator for the State of Massachusetts. Prior to this, Kennedy had served in the U.S. House of Representatives. In 1960, he defeated Nixon and brought new hope and direction for a country undergoing social changes.

After his inaugural address, *New York Magazine* hailed Kennedy as one of the great spokesmen of his time.

Notes
_____
_____
_____
_____
_____
_____
_____
_____
_____
_____
_____
_____
_____
_____
_____
_____
_____
_____
_____

Identifying the Purpose of a Presentation

Introduction   To plan an effective presentation, you need to determine its purpose.

To help determine the purpose of your presentation, you should ask yourself the following questions.

- Why this specific presentation?
- What should the participants be able to do or understand at the completion of the presentation?
- How should the participants react at the end of the presentation?

Sample purpose statements   The following purpose statements illustrate the reason, outcome, and skills that a presentation should communicate.

A sales representative might describe the purpose this way:

> *I want to make my customers feel comfortable about their buying decisions. I want them to feel enthusiastic about ordering my product. I want to make sure the product is accepted.*

A manager might want to inform a small group of new changes and describe the purpose this way:

> *I want to review next year's budget and receive input on some changes. This would enable everyone to begin the new year with the same objectives.*

A division manager might want to motivate a large audience and describe the purpose this way:

> *I want to recognize the individuals who met or exceeded their goals. I want to excite them about next year's goals and incentives. I will give them competitive information to help them achieve their new goals.*

Program Exercise: The Purpose Statement

Directions   Write a purpose statement for your presentation using the material discussed.

Why   _____

_____

_____

_____

_____

_____

_____

_____

_____

What   _____

_____

_____

_____

_____

_____

_____

_____

_____

How   _____

_____

_____

_____

_____

_____

_____

_____

Analyzing the Audience

Introduction   Analyzing the audience enables you to speak directly to your audience's needs and experience.

Audience analysis topics   When analyzing your audience you need to explore the following topics:

- Determine the number of participants.
- Verify the participants' roles and responsibilities.
- Discover the participants' attention level. A low attention level increases the need attention-getting techniques.
- Identify the audience's objectives and priorities.
- Research the topics required to achieve these objectives.
- Identify the level of detail required.
- Select the overall presentation method.
- Choose the format.

Benefits of audience analysis   Audience analysis during the planning stage can help you in the following ways:

- Identify the audience's key business objectives;
- Determine the audience's present level of performance;
- Identify the overall business climate;
- Allow the presenter to project an appropriate personality or style;
- Determine the appropriate format; and
- Increase the presenter's comfort level.

How to get audience information   There are many ways to get information about your potential audience.

- Speak to the participants before the presentation.
- Send out a questionnaire or preparatory reading materials.
- Speak to coworkers or managers.
- Perform market research.
- Compare similar groups.
- Introduce yourself to the participants as they enter the room.
- Ask questions during the presentation to stimulate feedback.
- Talk to the participants after the presentation to verify that the proper message was received.

Program Exercise: Audience Analysis

Directions   Fill in the blanks and check off the items that describe your audience.

1. Presentation Objectives

   As a result of my presentation, I want my audience to: _____

   _____

   _____

   _____

2. Detailed Audience Analysis

   The audience's knowledge of the subject is:

   ❏ Extremely knowledgeable

   ❏ Generally knowledgeable

   ❏ Narrowly knowledgeable

   ❏ Ignorant of subject matter

   ❏ Unknown

   The audience's opinions about the subject matter are:

   ❏ Very favorable

   ❏ Favorable

   ❏ Neutral

   ❏ Slightly hostile

   ❏ Hostile

   ❏ Unknown

   The audience's opinions about the trainer are:

   ❏ Very favorable

   ❏ Favorable

   ❏ Neutral

   ❏ Slightly hostile

   ❏ Hostile

   ❏ Unknown

The audience's opinions about your company are:

❏ Very favorable

❏ Favorable

❏ Neutral

❏ Slightly hostile

❏ Hostile

❏ Unknown

3. Audience Attitudes

The audience's reason(s) for attending this presentation: _____

_____

_____

_____

4. Overall Audience Analysis

Number of participants attending the session:

❏ 0–10

❏ 11–15

❏ 16–20

❏ 21–25

❏ 26 or more

Audience relationship to presenter:

❏ Customers

❏ Managers

❏ Peers

❏ Subordinates

❏ Public

❏ Other

Length of time the presenter and audience have known each other:

- ❑ New
- ❑ Less than one year
- ❑ 1–2 years
- ❑ More than 2 years
- ❑ Unknown

The audience's understanding of subject vocabulary:

- ❑ Technical
- ❑ Non-technical
- ❑ Generally high
- ❑ Generally low
- ❑ Unknown

5. Presentation Approach

The technique most likely to gain the attention of my audience is:

- ❑ Example/analogy
- ❑ Experience
- ❑ Testimony
- ❑ Demonstration
- ❑ Challenge
- ❑ Statistics
- ❑ Mixture
- ❑ Other _____

6. Other Vital Information:

_____

_____

_____

_____

_____

MODULE 2:
Preparing the Presentation
UNIT 1
Organizing the Information
Overview

Introduction   Once you have completed your planning activities, analyzed your audience, and selected the presentation method and tools, you are ready to prepare the presentation.

Preparing the presentation means organizing your topics into the following categories:

- attention getters;

- the introduction;

- the body; and

- the closing.

Unit objectives   When you complete this unit, you will be able to:

- write at least three attention getters;

- write a draft of an introduction;

- write a draft of a body; and

- write a draft of a closing.

Topics   This unit describes the main parts of a presentation and the guidelines for organizing the information. The topics include:

- Developing Attention Getters;

- Developing the Introduction;

- Preparing the Body of Your Presentation; and

- Preparing the Closing of Your Presentation.

Developing Attention Getters

Introduction

To make an effective presentation, you need to:

- get the participants' interest right away;
- tell them what they will hear or do; and
- explain how they can benefit from your presentation.

Plan to use attention getters in *various parts* of your presentation to maintain the participants' interest.

Attention getters

Attention getters are techniques used to focus the participants on the information being delivered.

Types of attention getters include:

- questions;
- stories;
- factual statements;
- illustrations;
- statistics;
- quotations; and
- jokes.

Developing the Introduction

The introduction The table below describes how to prepare an effective introduction. These are guidelines for you to consider when preparing the introduction of your presentation.

Table 2.1.1: How to Prepare an Introduction

Step		Description
Step 1.	Manage the participants' expectations	• Preview what will be covered in the presentation. This avoids potential confusion on the part of the participants.
Step 2.	Highlight the objectives and benefits	• Describe the end result of the presentation. Tell the participants what they should know and/or be able to do at the end of the presentation. • Highlight how the knowledge or skill being presented will be of advantage to them.
Step 3.	Build credibility	• Describe your background/experience, your sources of information, and any insights you have on the subject matter.
Step 4.	Introduce presenter and participants	• Briefly introduce yourself to the audience. Describe your role, experience, and other relevant information. Provide the same type of information when you introduce a guest presenter. • If the group is small and the participants are unacquainted with each other, ask the participants to briefly introduce themselves to the group.
Step 5.	Discuss logistical issues	• Describe specific logistical information relevant to this presentation. For example, handouts to be distributed and the scheduled meeting time frame.

Preparing the Body of Your Presentation

Introduction   The body of your presentation contains the central message you are trying to convey.

The body   The table below describes how to prepare an effective body. These are guidelines for you to consider when preparing the body of your presentation.

Table 2.1.2: How to Prepare the Body of Your Presentation

Step		Description
Step 1.	Limit the body to three major points	• It is important to keep your message focused. This is essential if you are to successfully achieve your goal within an appropriate time frame. • The body of the presentation can include subtopics.
Step 2.	Do not overload the participant with nice-to-know information	• Only include information that supports your key points. For example, cite references and statistics as part of the body of the presentation. • Omit information that can potentially confuse and distract the participants' attention.
Step 3.	Provide clear, current, and non-biased support	• The body should include information which persuades the participants to a new idea or course of action. Use objective information to strengthen your point of view.
Step 4.	Use transitions between topics	• Explain to the participants when you are moving from one topic to another. This approach guides the participant along the different points, preventing confusion and loss of attention. Transitions help the entire group stay focused.

Preparing the Closing of Your Presentation

Introduction The closing is often rushed or omitted altogether when presenters take too much time delivering their presentation. The closing should restate the key points of the presentation and outline a plan of action.

The closing The table below describes how to prepare an effective closing. These are guidelines for you to consider when preparing the closing of your presentation.

Table 2.1.3: How to Prepare the Closing of Your Presentation

Step		Description
Step 1.	Restate the objectives	• Restating the objectives allows you to reinforce the key points.
Step 2.	Summarize key points	• Outline the important topics that were presented. • Include participants' comments that may have supported your major topics.
Step 3.	Conclude with an action plan	• An action plan consists of activities that the participants perform to help them recall the key points of the presentation.

UNIT 2
Preparing the Presentation Material
Overview

Introduction

Visual aids are used as a vehicle for delivering your information. In a study performed at University of Wisconsin, visual aids increased vocabulary learning by 200%. At Columbia University, visual aids increased retention by 14–38%. The University of Minnesota found that visuals can reduce the amount of time required to present a concept by 40%.*

Some visual aids require preparation in advance, while others form an interactive part of the presentation.

EXAMPLE: you can prepare a 35mm slide presentation and use a flip chart to record the participants' comments.

Knowing when and how to use these tools increases your credibility as a presenter.

Unit objectives

When you complete this unit, you will be able to:

- identify the guidelines for selecting visual aids.

Topics

This unit covers the following topics:

- Selecting Visual Aids—Guidelines.

---

* Results quoted in Cothran, T. (1989). The value of visuals: A special report. *TRAINING*.

Selecting Visual Aids—Guidelines

Introduction   Before determining the appropriate type of visual aid for your presentation, consider the following:

- your presentation goals;
- your budget;
- the room size/configuration;
- your equipment experience; and
- the number of visuals.

Presentation goals   Identify the results you expect to achieve. Use visuals that target and reinforce the message of your presentation.

Budget   Keep the production of visual aids within your budget. You may want to produce a video but only have the funds for a slide show.

Make use of local resources when producing your visuals. Locate a copy or printing company and find out what services they can provide. For example, bring in a sketch or illustration and ask about the types of color transparencies they can produce.

Room size/ configuration   Choose visual aids according to the room size and layout in which you will give your presentation. Be sure to consider the number of people in your audience.

Equipment experience   Make sure you are comfortable using the visual aid. Explore the uses of presentation equipment before building the presentation. Practice your presentation with the visual aids to eliminate any technical problems.

Number of visuals   Deciding on the appropriate number of visuals depends on the length of your presentation, its purpose, and the number of points that need emphasis.

EXAMPLE: If your presentation is highly technical, you may need many visuals to illustrate your subject matter. If your objective is to motivate a group of coworkers, a single graphic or cartoon may be all that you need.

Video Exercise: One-to-One Presentation

Background
Donald, a sales representative for AmCor Copiers, has prepared a presentation to be given to Robin the chairperson for the purchasing equipment committee. Robin and Donald have met before to discuss her copier requirements.

Directions
1. Observe Donald's presentation skills. Recall the topics you have learned in this workshop to evaluate Donald's presentation to Robin. These include:

   - The Purpose Statement;

   - Audience Analysis;

   - Attention Getters;

   - The Introduction;

   - The Body;

   - The Conclusion; and

   - Participant's Comfort.

2. List at least three situations where Donald's presentation skills are effective:

   _____

   _____

   _____

   _____

   _____

3. List at least three situations where Donald's presentation skills need improvement.

   _____

   _____

   _____

   _____

   _____

   _____

Notes
   _____

   _____

   _____

   _____

   _____

Program Exercise: Preparing Your Presentation

Directions Use your Audience Analysis Worksheet and the information in this unit to begin planning your presentation. Be prepared to give the first five minutes of your presentation after completing this worksheet.

Purpose _____
_____
_____

Method _____
_____
_____

Attention getters _____
_____
_____

Introduction _____
_____
_____
_____

Body

Main Points	Supporting Information
1.	
2.	
3.	

Conclusion _____
_____
_____
_____

Visual aids _____
_____
_____
_____

Room Environment

**1. Room Layout
(sketch at right)**

```
┌─────────────────────────────────┐
│                                 │
│                                 │
│                                 │
│                                 │
│                                 │
│                                 │
│                                 │
└─────────────────────────────────┘
```

2. Equipment _____
_____
_____

**3. Participant
     Comfort** _____
_____
_____
_____

MODULE 3:
The Delivery
UNIT 1
Preparing and Using Visual Aids
Overview

Introduction   Visual aids contribute style and depth while emphasizing the main points of an effective presentation. The use of visual aids helps you communicate your message to the participant. Visuals increase both the participants' understanding and retention of the material being presented.

Unit objectives   When you complete this unit, you will be able to:

- prepare visual aids; and

- demonstrate use of visual aids.

Topics   This unit covers guidelines and tips for the following visual aid topics:

- Designing Visual Aids—Guidelines;

- Visual Formats;

- The Overhead Projector;

- The 35mm Slide Projector;

- The Videotape;

- Sample Forms and Handouts;

- The White Board; and

- The Flip Chart.

Designing Visual Aids—Guidelines

Introduction   Once you choose the visual aids, you need to consider how to use the following:

- level of detail;
- design consistency;
- 6 x 6 rule; and
- use of color.

Effective use of the above will increase the participants' interest and anticipation.

Level of detail   Omit all unnecessary details in your diagrams or illustrations. A stylized visual allows participant to focus on the key points.

Design consistency   Design consistency means that the design elements (fonts, colors, and position) are use consistently from one visual to another. This approach allows the participant to focus o the message being delivered.

6 x 6 rule   Limit visuals to 6 words across and 6 lines down. This approach allows for adequate "white space." White space is the empty space which surrounds your text and/or graphics. This white space improves the readability of the information contained in the visual.

Color   Limit visuals to two or three colors. Too many colors detract from the message.

Following is a list of recommended colors for business visuals:

- green;
- blue;
- black; and
- red.

NOTE:	Restrict the use of red to highlight numbers which show a deficit.

Visual Formats

Introduction
Visual aids can use any of several formats or layouts. Formats for visual aids include:

- lists;
- tables;
- charts;
- diagrams;
- photographs/maps; and
- cartoons.

Lists
Lists should not contain more than 7–9 items in each group. Be sure that lists are clearly labeled.

Tables
Tables can effectively:

- organize material;
- delineate procedures; and
- compare and contrast similar information.

Charts
Charts can be easily generated using a personal computer and a spreadsheet program. Your local copy center may be able to generate charts for you if you do not have access to a computer.

Some common types include:

- bar;
- pie;
- area; and
- alpine line charts.

Diagrams
Diagrams should focus on the essentials and not include too much detail.

Photographs/maps
Photographs and maps can provide the detail you may need to express your message. A photograph can have a strong emotional impact on your audience. We are all familiar with photographs of disaster areas—without any words these photographs convey a powerful message.

Cartoons
Cartoons can be used to simulate human interactions or bring out a point with humor.

The Overhead Projector

Introduction   The overhead projector is the most frequently used visual aid in business. Below are the advantages, disadvantages, and tips for using the overhead projector.

Table 3.1.1: Advantages and Disadvantages of the Overhead Projector

Advantages	Disadvantages
• Inexpensive	• Requires electricity
• Easy to create and operate	• Limits view of certain participants
• Portable	• Can be noisy (older models)
• Color transparencies readily available	• Quality of transparency degenerates over time

Preparation tips   When preparing your overheads, consider the following tips:

- Use with groups of 5 to 25 people.
- Mount on frames.
- Place your notes on the border of the frame.
- Use large print.
- Observe the 6 x 6 rule.
- Number the transparencies.
- Make sure you know how to change the bulb.
- Have an extra bulb handy.
- Use color transparencies.

Presentation tips   When presenting your overheads, consider the following tips:

- Focus the first transparency *before* you begin.
- Use the overlay technique to develop anticipation.
- Lay a pen on the projector as a pointer.
- Use masking tape on the projector. This blocks any unnecessary light.
- Project onto a flip chart pad when no screen is available.
- When demonstrating how to complete a form, use a flip chart and the projector. Project the form onto the flip chart and demonstrate how to complete the form by writing on the flip chart.
- Turn off the projector during overhead changes.
- Move away from the projector when not changing the overhead.

The 35mm Slide Projector

Introduction

The 35mm slide projector is one of the most professional visual-aid tools used for business presentations. Below are the advantages, disadvantages, and tips for using a slide projector.

Table 3.1.2: Advantages and Disadvantages of the Slide Projector

Advantages	Disadvantages
• Easy to operate • Portable • Interchangeable slides • Accommodates large groups • High visual appeal	• Requires electricity • Costly to produce • May require a darkened room • May make note taking difficult for participants • Can be noisy (older models) • Rearranging the order of the slides is difficult during the presentation

Preparation tips

When preparing your slides, consider the following tips:

- Use with groups of 5 or more.
- Limit the slide show to 20 minutes.
- Limit the number of words on a slide to the 6 x 6 rule.
- Plan to add value to the slides with your comments.
- Number the slides.
- Use two projectors to compare or contrast key topics.
- Make custom slides for special audiences (company logo, etc.).
- Transfer 35mm photographs to slides.
- Learn how to change the bulb.
- Have an extra bulb available.

Presentation tips

When presenting your slides, consider the following tips:

- Focus the projector *before* the presentation.
- Tape the remote control down to a table.
- Place the projector up front and under a table with a wide-angle zoom lens. When you place the projector in the front of the room, you are less likely to require a darkened room.

The Videotape

Introduction

The videotape has revolutionized the visual-aid industry by providing a relatively low-cost way to deliver a presentation. Videotape production is a multibillion dollar industry. Below are the advantages, disadvantages, and tips for using videotapes.

Table 3.1.3: Advantages and Disadvantages of the Videotape

Advantages	Disadvantages
• Can be reviewed easily	• Bulky equipment
• Many titles/subjects available	• Significant set-up time
• Does not require a darkened room	• Different formats (Beta, VHS, PAL)

Preparation tips

When preparing your videotape, consider the following tips:

- Do not use the video as a replacement for the presenter.

- Plan specific topics as part of a discussion after viewing. A group debriefing ensures that the key points are understood.

- Have extra copies of videotapes made.

- Consider renting production videos or feature films to use as attention getters or to illustrate key points.

Presentation tips

When presenting the video, consider the following tips:

- Test all equipment a few hours before the presentation.

- To encourage discussion, stop the videotape after key points.

- Be enthusiastic and a model of attention when viewing the videotape.

Sample Forms and Handouts

Introduction Distributing sample forms and handouts during a presentation is a traditional but effective technique. The most important reason for using sample forms and handouts is to maintain the attention of your audience. Below are the advantages, disadvantages, and tips for using handouts.

Table 3.1.4: Advantages and Disadvantages of Sample Forms and Handouts

Advantages	Disadvantages
• Provides an outline, a focus for the presentation • Reduces the need to take notes • Provides material participants can read after the presentation • Emphasizes the key points	• Time consuming to prepare and update • Multiple handouts can be overwhelming to both the participants and the presenter

Preparation tips When preparing your handouts, consider the following tips:

- Copy handouts on three-hole paper and store them in a binder.
- Leave white space for notes.
- Limit the number of handouts to the important topics.

Presentation tips When distributing your handouts, consider the following tips:

- Inform the audience that handouts will be distributed.
- Distribute handouts only when the topic is about to be discussed.
- Start distributing handouts from more than one place in the room.
- Allow participants enough time to look at the handouts. This increases the probability that they will read the material after the presentation.

The White Board

Introduction

The white board is another popular visual aid that is found in the majority of business settings. Below are the advantages, disadvantages, and tips for using the white board.

Table 3.1.5: Advantages and Disadvantages of the White Board

Advantages	Disadvantages
• Readily available	• Handwriting may be hard to read
• Easy to erase	• Back is turned to audience—may appear to be talking to the board
• Accommodates color	
• Allows participant input	

Preparation tips

When preparing a presentation that incorporates the use of a white board consider the following tips:

- Bring your own white board markers, cleaner, and eraser.

- Sketch out any complicated diagrams on a piece of paper or index card.

Presentation tips

When using a white board, consider the following presentation tips:

- Use white board (dry-erase) markers.

- Stand to the side when writing.

- Put the marker down after writing.

NOTE:	If you use the wrong type of marker on a white board, you may be able to erase it using this procedure. Completely cover anything you have written on the board with white board markers (dry-erase). Rub thoroughly with a white board eraser.

The Flip Chart

Introduction

The flip chart is popular because of its low cost and ease-of-use. Below are the advantages, disadvantages, and tips for using the flip chart.

Table 3.1.6: Advantages and Disadvantages of the Flip Chart

Advantages	Disadvantages
• Readily available • Inexpensive • Accommodates color • Allows participant input • Easy-to-use • Can be reused • Transportable	• Handwriting may be hard to read • Back is turned to audience—may appear to be talking to the flip chart

Preparation tips

When preparing a presentation that incorporates the use of a flip chart consider the following tips:

- Use a flip chart with groups of 25 or less.
- Pencil your notes lightly next to key points on the flip chart.
- Prepare your text in advance by using a pencil to lightly trace the text on the flip chart page. When that topic is discussed, simply write over the existing penciled text.
- Use three-inch lettering.
- Use the 6 x 6 rule.
- Write on every other page. Tape the written page and the following blank page together. This prevents bleed-through.
- Use different colors to highlight key words.

Presentation tips

When using a flip chart, consider the following tips:

- Use colored markers.
- Stand to the side when writing.
- Put the marker down after writing.
- Use two flip charts. Use one for prepared material and a second for writing participant's comments.
- When using the flip chart to recap a session or brainstorm, tape pages to the wall.

Unit 2
Using Effective Presentation Skills—The Basics
Overview

Introduction   As a presenter, most of the attention is focused on you—what you are saying and how you are delivering your message. To be an effective communicator you must use presentation skills that promote a coordinated presentation. Even a well-organized presentation with appealing visual aids can fail to reach its objectives if the presenter's delivery style is not effective.

Unit objectives   When you complete this unit, you will be able to:

- complete a ten-minute presentation; and

- demonstrate the effective use of three of the following:

  - vocal techniques;

  - non-verbal communication; and

  - control of nervousness and anxiety.

Topics   This unit describes the main parts of a presentation and the guidelines for organizing the information. The topics include:

- Using Effective Vocal Skills;

- Using Non-Verbal Communication Techniques;

- Controlling Nervousness and Anxiety; and

- Dealing with Difficult Questions—Guidelines.

35

Using Effective Vocal Skills

Introduction   Effective vocal techniques include:

- speed;
- volume;
- pitch; and
- quality.

Speed   Speed is the rate at which you communicate the message to the audience.

A successful presenter:

- speaks at a moderate pace and uses pauses effectively. Speaking too quickly tires and frustrates your audience, speaking too slowly bores and can frustrate your audience;
- avoids using filler word such as "um" and "uh"; and
- controls speed by using pauses (silent) and eye contact.

Volume   The optimum volume depends on these factors:

- the size of the room; and
- the size of your audience.

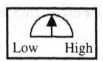

A successful presenter:

- speaks loudly enough for the people furthest back to hear but not too loud for the people in the front row; and
- varies the volume from soft to loud for a more interesting voice.

Pitch   Pitch is the tone or the inflection in your voice. Use the tone in your voice to emphasize specific points in your presentation. For example, newscasters change their tone to emphasize important words or phrases.

A successful presenter:

- varies the tone for a more interesting voice.

Quality   Vocal quality is the overall sound of your voice.

A successful presenter:

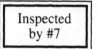

- employs warm, rich, pleasant, and powerful tones; and
- pronounces words correctly and clearly enunciates all words.

Using Nonverbal Communication Techniques

Introduction
Nonverbal communication means sending messages to the audience without using words. For example, using strong hand gestures to emphasize an important point sends a powerful nonverbal message to your audience.

Your goal is to combine both vocal techniques and nonverbal communication techniques in a coordinated presentation.

Non-verbal techniques include:

- eye contact;
- facial expression;
- appearance;
- hand gestures; and
- posture.

Eye contact

Eye-to-eye contact is an important factor in nonverbal communication. Eye contact promotes confidence and security between the presenter and the audience.

A successful presenter:

- makes eye contact lasting four to five seconds;
- makes random eye contact with individuals in a small group; and
- identifies a focus group within a larger group.

Appearance

Successful business dress means not making your appearance an issue. The focus of attention should be on the message not the messenger. For example, an *inappropriate* tie or scarf may distract the participants' attention from your message.

A successful presenter:

- matches his/her appearance with the audience. Dressing a bit above the audience is appropriate;
- wears less jewelry; and
- checks his/her appearance before the presentation.

Facial expression

Your facial expression communicates both direct and subtle messages to your audience.

A successful presenter uses expressions appropriate:

- to the audience; and

- to the topic.

A serious topic requires a serious facial expression. A presenter should generate warmth by smiling to indicate his/her pleasure in speaking.

Hand gestures

Hand gestures create visual images for your audience to follow. Watch your hand gestures when you practice your presentation in front of the mirror.

A successful presenter:

- uses gestures appropriate to the audience;

- does not fidget;

- uses hand gestures that are generally above the waist; and

- uses gestures to draw attention to key points.

Posture

Your posture reflects the impression you want to send to your audience.

A successful presenter:

- communicates high energy and confidence;

- keeps hands out of pockets and stands straight without looking posed; and

- makes sure his/her posture is appropriate to the topic.

Controlling Nervousness and Anxiety

Introduction Nervousness and anxiety are symptoms of stress. People act differently to stressful situations. Some individuals react expressively and emotionally while other individuals react inwardly and are quiet. This phenomenon is commonly known as "fight or flight."

Overcoming Stress Use the table below to assist you if you are experiencing nervousness or anxiety.

Table 3.2.1: How to Overcome Stress

Stress Symptom	Counter Measure
Dry mouth	• Drink tea with honey and plenty of other fluids. • Do not drink coffee. • Abstain from alcohol the night before and day of the presentation. • Request a pitcher of water for your presentation.
Biting lips	• Inhale through your nose and exhale through your mouth. • Practice speaking in front of a mirror and observe your mouth. • Articulate your words clearly.
Squeaky voice	• Breathe in slowly through your nose and count to five. Exhale and count backwards. • Gargle with a carbonated beverage.
Nervous, clammy hands	• Shake your hands out loosely before the presentation. • Avoid using pointers. • Press fingertips firmly on the table while speaking. • Rub hands with talcum powder before the presentation. • Do not hold anything in your hands.
Pacing/Rocking	• Stop moving whenever you pause. • Use more than one visual. • Place your body weight forward on your toes.

continued on next page

Table 3.2.1: How to Overcome Stress, *continued*

Stress Symptom	Counter Measure
Forgetfulness	• Concentrate on every word you are saying. • Take a break to collect yourself. • Give the participants a question to discuss. • Practice and know your material.
Nervousness	• Practice! Practice! Practice! • Rehearse your presentation before a non-judgmental group. • Release excess energy before your presentation. • Meet with participants informally before the presentation. • Maintain a positive mental attitude. • Breathe in slowly through your nose and count to five. Exhale and count backwards. • Do not apologize to your audience.

Program Exercise: A 10 Minute Presentation

Directions

1. Complete a ten minute presentation. As the presenter plan to demonstrate the following Basic Presentation Skills:

   - Vocal Skills;

   - Non-Verbal Communication; and

   - Controlling Nervousness and Anxiety.

2. Plan the timing of your presentation so that you are *finished* within a 30 second "window." In other words, you should be finished between nine minutes and thirty seconds and ten minutes and thirty seconds of your start time.

NOTE:	Designate a person to signal you at different time intervals. For example, signal five minutes remaining, two minutes remaining.

3. As a member of the audience you should follow these guidelines.

   - You are neutral toward the presenter and the topic.

   - Allow the presenter to get through the material being presented.

   - Ask and answer questions.

   - Be prepared to provide specific feedback to the presenter.

   - Use the evaluation forms provided by your instructor to provide feedback.

4. Provide feedback.

   - As a group, list three situations where you felt the individual did well.

   - As a group, list three situations where you felt the individual could improve.

   - Hand the feedback forms to the presenter.

IMPORTANT:	The goal of this exercise is to provide a neutral situation to allow the presenter to practice the basic presentation skills.

Dealing with Difficult Questions—Guidelines

Introduction   Use the following guidelines when you are faced with difficult questions from the participants.

Table 3.2.2: Strategies for Handling Difficult Questions

Strategy	Description
Listen with an open mind	• Demonstrate non-defensive behavior and use non-judgmental comments.
Pause	• Collect your thoughts. • Allow the participant to say more if appropriate. • Relieve any tension.
Clarify the situation	• Paraphrase the participant's remark to make sure you clearly understand the question or viewpoint. • Get an understanding of the critical issue or concern before saying the first thought that comes to mind.
Accept the input	• Indicate the individual's right to have a particular point of view. You do not have to agree with the participant's comments. The goal is to understand the participant's view, not to get agreement on what is being said.
Remain objective	• Don't react emotionally or act threatened. • Keep your response focused on facts.
Address the group	• Restate your views or answer the concern or question. • Accept the fact that not everyone will always agree with your viewpoint. • State your response to the entire group—not to an individual.
Check that the question has been addressed	• Ask the participant if the question has been adequately explained and move to the next topic.

Video Exercise: Presenting to a Group

Background In an earlier video we saw Donald making a presentation to Robin who is the chairperson of the purchasing equipment committee.

In this video Robin has prepared a presentation for the purchasing committee to review Donald's proposal.

Directions 1. Observe Robin's presentation skills. Recall the topics you have learned in this module to evaluate her presentation to the purchasing committee.

- Use of Visuals
- Vocal Skills
- Non-Verbal Communication
- Nervousness and Anxiety
- Difficult Questions

2. List at least three situations where Robin's presentation skills are effective:

_____

_____

_____

_____

_____

3. List at least three situations where Robin's presentation skills need improvement.

_____

_____

_____

_____

_____

Notes _____

_____

_____

_____

Program Exercise: Difficult Situations—A 10 Minute Presentation

Directions

1. Complete a ten minute presentation. As the presenter plan to demonstrate the following presentation skills:

    *   Vocal Skills;

    *   Non-Verbal Communication; and

    *   Controlling Nervousness and Anxiety.

2. All questions asked must be answered at the time they are asked. Plan to adjust your presentation to accommodate different questions and situations.

NOTE:	Designate a person to signal you at different time intervals. For example, signal five minutes remaining, two minutes remaining.

3. As a member of the audience you should follow these guidelines:

    *   You have strong views toward the presenter and the topic.

    *   Allow the presenter to get through the material being presented.

    *   Ask a maximum of two difficult questions per person.

    *   Use non-verbal communication techniques to indicate disapproval over a specific topic during the presentation.

    *   Be prepared to provide specific feedback to the presenter.

4. Provide feedback.

    *   As a group, list three situations where you felt the individual did well.

    *   As a group, list three situations where you felt the individual could improve.

    *   Hand feedback forms back to the presenter.

IMPORTANT:	The goal of this exercise is to provide the presenter some practice handling difficult situations. All situations in this exercise should reflect acceptable business meeting behavior.

Video Exercise: Presenting to a Large Group

Background
This video takes place at the AmCor's Annual Sales Meeting and shows two types of presentations: a large group presentation and an impromptu presentation. Both of these types of situations can be nerve-wracking.

The executive has prepared for this annual sales meeting and will be using a few 35mm slides in the presentation. Donald will be asked to give an impromptu presentation.

Directions
Observe these two types of presentations. Recall the topics you have learned in this workshop to evaluate these presentations.

Notes

_____

_____

_____

_____

_____

_____

_____

_____

_____

_____

_____

_____

_____

_____

_____

_____

_____

_____

_____

_____

_____

_____

APPENDIX

Table of Contents

Program Exercise: Preparing Your Presentation

Directions   Use your Audience Analysis Worksheet and the information in this unit to begin planning your presentation. Be prepared to give the first five minutes of your presentation after completing this worksheet.

Purpose   To convince the purchasing committee to reverse its decision of not ordering a color copier system and to accept the idea of leasing a color copier.

Method   I hope to do this through group discussion, by providing factual information and using the committee support I already have.

Attention getters
- Solution we failed to look at in past
- Lease vs. purchase
- Save over $16,000 in the course of a year by leasing vs. outside activities
- Non-binding lease

Introduction   Good Morning. During our last meeting, we discussed in great detail, the problems we have been having with our current copier system. I have discussed the topic with our copier people and have a solution that we failed to look at! Let's review our needs as discussed in our last meeting.

Body

Main Points		Supporting Information
1.	We still have color copying needs	• review color requirements • current spending for outside services
2.	Lease can actually save us budget dollars	• current spending vs. lease cost • total yearly savings
3.	Does not require a major commitment on our part	• non-binding • can purchase when we want • can resume outside services

---

Conclusion   The risk involved is minimal in relation to the yearly dollars saved. We have an offer for a lease with an option to buy. This will enable us to save money currently spent which can be applied to the purchase of a color copier system. I would like to go ahead with the proposal. Please read the proposal and call me if your have any questions.

Visual aids

Room Environment   Room Layout (sketch the room layout below):

ITC Assistance Line

As part of this workshop, the following free service is available:

- An evaluation of your presentation. Send a video or audio tape of your presentation to International Training Corporation 357 Winston Avenue NE, North Canton, Ohio 44720. We will be happy to evaluate your presentation and offer constructive feedback. This service is available for one year from postdate of registration form.

You must send a completed registration form to be eligible for this complementary service.

Contact International Training Corporation at 216–966–1170. Please do not contact Pfeiffer & Company in regard to this assistance line.

We also provide assistance and consulting services in designing and presenting your material. Please call us for details.

Workshop Evaluation Form

Directions Please complete the evaluation form below. *Thank you* for your feedback on this workshop.

Company: _____ Date: _____

Instructor: _____

		Very Effective	Effective	Needs More Attention	Comments
Administrator	Knowledge of Course Material				
	Organization of Information				
	Presentation Skills				
Visual Aids	Quality of Visual Aids				
Practice Exercises	Program Exercises				
	Video Exercises				
Other	Participant Guide				

Remarks _____

_____

_____

_____

_____

ITC Assistance Line Registration Form

Name: _____

Home Address: _____

_____

Home Telephone: _____

Work Telephone: _____

Mail to:
International Training Corp.
357 Winston Avenue, NE
North Canton, Ohio 44720
Attn: Assistance Line